Is Society Holding 'The Smoking Gun' When it Comes to Mass School Shootings?

Meagin Colson, MA

Contents

Parents, policy makers, and politicians alike have been debating gun control legislation as a means to prevent mass school shootings ever since the Columbine High School massacre in 1999. However, this type of reactionary logic only attempts to partially control for one of the many complicated variables involved in these events and simultaneously ignores the underlying causes of these tragedies. "The whole is greater than the sum of its parts." This great quote describes why reductionistic thinking, such as zooming in on any one factor, is an ineffective approach to solving complex problems. It is only when we understand how the elements are related to each other that that nature of the problem emerges. This book offers a theoretical framework on identifying the origin of the problem and reconciling the issue, instead, from the ground up. The etiology of the mass

school shooting phenomenon is explained from a brief

review of the research into psychological learning

systems and how they interact with societal norms to

predict behavior. The findings provide an understanding

of how deteriorating cultural values ultimately play a

systematic role in mass school shooting incidents. The

framework outlined can also be applied across the board

to all social issues on a macro-level. The book concludes

by making suggestions for future research and

recommends solutions to thwart future mass school

shooting incidents.

Chapter 1: Introduction

In February 2018, the nation experienced yet another mass school shooting that left 17 students and staff members of a Florida high school dead and more than 15 injured. The suspect was a 19-year-old, disgruntled, prior student of the school. The incident prompted gun control debates on every local and national news network. From a limited perspective, gun control may appear to be a logical solution to a very complex problem; however, it is not rational to think that passing legislation to limit gun ownership is the fix-all answer, especially considering that murder is illegal, a law that all mass-murderers are breaking despite their weapon of choice. Guns have been around since 1364 (American Firearms Institute, n.d.); however, school shootings have only recently become a widespread epidemic. Why? To accurately understand and effectively counter this deep-seated issue of humanity with a proper strategy, it is imperative to identify its roots and work to eradicate it from its source.

"Cain killed Able with a rock. We have a <u>heart</u> problem, not a gun problem." This quote begs the question: **Is the decline in cultural values responsible for mass school shootings?** And if so, do we need to turn our focus for a solution away from political leaders and toward ourselves as a society?

The purpose of this research is to explain how society has evolved to include such high instances of mass school shooting events. School shootings are all too often experienced yet the intrinsic essence of the problem remains unexplained. Extremely violent behavior is a complex phenomenon that occurs when multiple risk factors and social forces converge (Gentile, Saleem, & Anderson, 2007; Bornstein, 2006); therefore a holistic perspective is required to explain these occurrences. This study provides a theoretical framework that demonstrates an interdisciplinary correlation between how theories born in social and behavioral psychology coalesce with how cultural values are conceptualized to determine behavioral outcomes. While certain key variables are shown to influence violent outcomes, it is important to note that the likelihood of a violent act increases proportionately with the number of risk factors present (Saner & Ellickson, 1996).

This study evaluates the overall well-being of our children by their reported levels of satisfaction, stress, and prevalence of mental illness – and how social environments influence their well-being. A review of applicable observational and cognitive psychological learning theories aids to establish an association between how children learn to operate in the world and the importance of cultural values. The study then focuses on deteriorating social issues that are most relevant to the topic and their cyclical relationship with the issue. The study concludes with a final assessment of the research, makes suggestions on areas of future research, and recommends solutions for reducing future school shooting instances. The implications of this study are broad and can be used to explain a wide range of other social issues.

Chapter 2: The Well-being of our Children

The first essential step in fully comprehending the problem in its entirety is gaining an understanding of the current state of our children. A review of self-reported survey data regarding well-being provides a vantage point from the adolescents' perspective. An ongoing study conducted by the Organisation for Economic Co-operation and Development (OECD) defines well-being as "the psychological, cognitive, social, and physical qualities that students need to live a happy and fulfilling life" (OECD, 2017). On the 2015 OECD PISA (Programme for International Student Assessment) survey, students were asked to rate their life satisfaction on a scale from 0 to 10, with 0 representing the worst possible life, and 10 representing the best possible life. In the United States, on average, students reported a level of 7.36 on the life-satisfaction scale. 35.9% of students reported they were very satisfied with life (a 9 or 10 on the scale) and a smaller, but not negligible, 11.8% of students reported they were not satisfied with life (0-4 on the scale) (OECD, 2017). The American Psychological Association's (APA) Stress in America survey found that teens report that their stress level during the school year far exceeds what they believe to be healthy (5.8 versus 3.9 on a 10-point scale) and tops adults average reported stress levels (5.8 for teens versus 5.1 for adults) (APA, 2014). See Chart 1, right. Many teens also reported

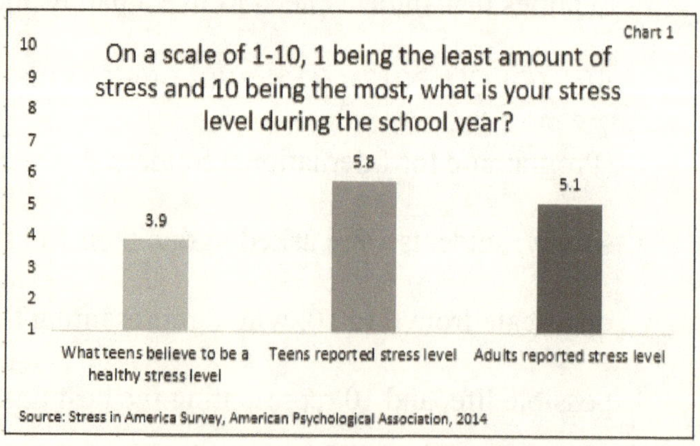

feeling overwhelmed (31%) and depressed or sad (30%)

as a result of stress. Despite their awareness of relatively

high self-reported levels of stress and associated

negative emotions, teens seem to underestimate the

potential impact that stress has on their physical and

mental health. Teens are more likely than adults to report

that their stress level has a slight or no impact on their

body or physical health (54% of teens versus 39% of

adults) or their mental health (52% of teens versus 43%

of adults) (APA, 2014) (Chart 2, left), despite copious amounts of available

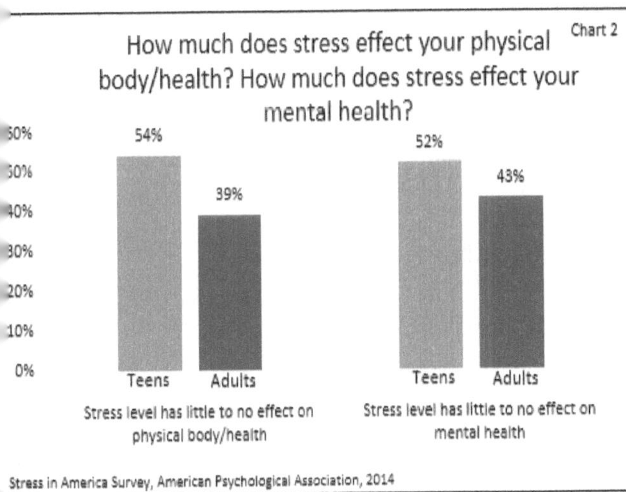

research to the contrary. For example, stress that is prolonged and managed poorly can result in negative physical, mental, and cognitive outcomes for youth (Steinberg, 2005). Experiencing high levels of stress or chronic stress can undermine physical health by increasing the likelihood of a weakened immune system, heart disease, obesity, and diabetes (Rosmond, 2005). Other negative outcomes include anxiety, depression, poor memory and language skills, and lower academic achievement (Farah, Nobel, & Hurt 2007). Since teens are indifferent to the physical and mental consequences of high stress levels, many do no regulate their emotions accordingly. In fact, over half of teens (55%) reported they are not doing enough to manage their stress, are not sure if they are doing enough to manage their stress, or never set aside time to manage stress (APA, 2014). Since stress is often a precursor to other mental illnesses, it is likely the underlying cause of many of the other mood and behavioral disorders seen in adolescents. According to the National Institute of Mental Health (NIH), in 2016, an estimated 49.5% of adolescents (aged 13-18) had a mental disorder and 22.2% experienced severe impairment ("Mental Illness," n.d.). Changes in cultural values and norms over time play a considerable role in the stress and affiliated mental health of today's youth. These shifts have substantially influenced the ways in which Americans raise their children, the values systems of adults and adolescents, and the socictal tolerance of certain behaviors – which, as the research will show, contribute to stress.

Before moving to a more complete discussion on deteriorating cultural values and the subsequent effects on adolescents, a brief examination into observational and cognitive learning theories will serve to adequately demonstrate the cyclical relationship between how behavior is learned through cognition, influenced by environmental factors, and displayed depending on situations and previously observed outcomes. These theories provide the foundational framework related to how societal norms are similarly integrated and the role they play in resulting behavior.

Chapter 3: Observational and Cognitive Learning Theories

Social-cognitive, information processing models focus on how people perceive, think, learn, and come to behave in particular ways. People's current behavioral tendencies result from past interactions with the social world; and behavior is modified based on perceived reactions and consequences. These social interactions may be real (e.g. parents, peers) or fictional (e.g. various forms of media) (Gentile et al., 2007).

Bandura's Social Learning Theory

During the 1960s, psychologist Albert Bandura conducted a series of classic experiments on observational learning, generally known as the Bobo doll experiments. The purpose of these studies was to determine if social behaviors were learned through

observation. Several variations of these experiments

were conducted but the basic premise remained. After

pre-testing children (between ages 3 and 6 years old) for

aggression levels, they were grouped with children with

similar levels of aggression and a lab experiment was

conducted where the independent variable was

manipulated in three conditions: (1) aggressive adult

model is shown to 24 children (acting aggressively

towards the Bobo doll in a distinctive manner – they

used a hammer in some cases, and in others threw the

doll in the air and shouted "Pow, Boom," (2) non-

aggressive adult model is shown to 24 children (played

in the room with them in a quiet and subdued manner,

ignoring the Bobo doll), and (3) no model shown

(control condition) to 24 children (played in the room,

not exposed to an adult model) (McLeod, 2014). The next stage in the experiment involved aggression arousal, where all the children (including the control group) were subjected to 'mild aggression arousal.' Each child was separately taken to a room with relatively attractive toys. As soon as the child started to play with the toys, the experimenter told the child that those were the experimenter's very best toys and she had decided to reserve them for the other children. In the final stage of the experiment, delayed imitation was tested. The child was then taken to another room which contained some aggressive toys (a mallet and peg board, dart guns, Bobo doll) and some non-aggressive toys (tea set, crayons, bears, plastic farm animals) and observed through a one-way mirror for 20 minutes. The results (which have been replicated many times by many researchers) showed that children who observed the aggressive model made far

more imitative aggressive responses than those who

were in the non-aggressive or control groups. There was

more partial and non-imitative aggression among those

children who had observed aggressive behavior,

although the difference for non-imitative aggression was

small. The girls in the aggressive model condition also

showed more physical aggressive responses if the model

was male, but more verbal aggressive responses if the

model was female – however, the exception to this

general pattern was the observation of how often they

punched Bobo, and in this case the effects of gender

were reversed. Boys were more likely to imitate same-

sex models than girls. Boys imitated more physically

aggressive acts than girls. There was little difference in

the verbal aggression between boys and girls (McLeod,

2014). These findings support what ultimately began Albert Bandura's Social Learning Theory, which concludes that people learn from one another through observation, imitation, and modeling and includes attention, memory, and motivation. A quote from Bandura states, "Most human behavior is learned observationally through modeling: from observing others, one forms an idea of how new behaviors are performed, and on later occasions this coded information serves as a guide for action." (McLeod, 2014). Social learning theory explains human behavior as a continuous reciprocal interaction between cognitive, behavioral, and environmental influences.

Cognitive-Neoassociation Theory

Cognitive-neoassociation theory states that numerous aversive events (e.g., frustration, provocations, loud noises, uncomfortable temperatures, and unpleasant odors) lead to negative affect and subsequently to aggression (Berkowitz, 1989, 1993). Through frequent associations, negative affect becomes linked to a variety of thoughts, memories, expressive motor reactions, and physiological responses. These responses are then automatically activated when negative affect is present in future circumstances and give rise to two immediate and simultaneous tendencies, fight or flight. The fight associations give rise to beginning stages of feelings of anger, whereas the flight associations give rise to beginning stages of feelings of fear. The tendency that is the stronger of the two is most likely to determine the individual's behavior in the present situation. Through classical conditioning, cues present in the current aversive event are likely to become associated with the experiences (e.g., thoughts, emotions, memories, and motor reactions). Similar cues in the future, even under different circumstances, are likely to trigger similar reactions and responses (Gentile et al., 2007).

General Aggression Model

The General Aggression Model (GAM) is a relatively new theory that integrates concepts and ideas from earlier models (Carnagey & Anderson, 2003; Anderson, Gentile, & Buckley, 2007). GAM describes a cyclical pattern of interaction between the person and their environment. The model is especially helpful in understanding how individual and situational variables affect a person's appraisal of a situation and ultimately affect the behavior performed in response to that appraisal. Input factors (personal and situational) are thought to influence an individual's present internal state, which consists of cognition, affect, and arousal. Each of these three routes can be influenced by input variables and can also influence one another. The present internal state then influences one's decision making process leading eventually to either a thoughtful action or an impulsive action. Impulsive actions and behaviors could be the result of immediate and spontaneous appraisals that are made without much thought or awareness. Thoughtful actions and behaviors, on the other hand, would be the result of searching for relevant information to re-evaluate the current circumstance, but this occurs only when given enough time and motivation to re-evaluate immediate appraisals. This does not mean thoughtful actions will be always nonaggressive and impulsive actions will be always aggressive. Both impulsive and thoughtful behaviors can be either aggressive or nonaggressive (Gentile et al., 2007).

<u>Chapter 4: Deteriorating Cultural Values and Societal Norms</u>

Cultural Values and Societal Norms defined

Cultural values and norms are informal and unregulated rules that define acceptable behavior within society. They provide social structure and an implied order of shared expectations. Each social situation involves a particular understanding of required conduct. As suggested in the learning theories discussed previously, norms are learned and reinforced throughout life by parents, teachers, mentors, peers, and others in the community. When social norms change, you can expect behavior patterns to change accordingly. And norms have certainly; albeit slowly in some instances, transformed over time. Think of the following examples and how they have changed over the past 40-50 years:

divorce, women in the workplace, women's clothing,

technology, television shows, respect for authority,

manners and civility, teen pregnancy and out of wedlock

births, religious affiliation. The American Values Survey

found that two-thirds of Americans think the country is

heading in the wrong direction and 69% believe the

country's values have deteriorated since the 1970s, citing

declining family values as a contributing factor (Cohn,

2012; Penn, 2012) (Chart 3). While all cultural values

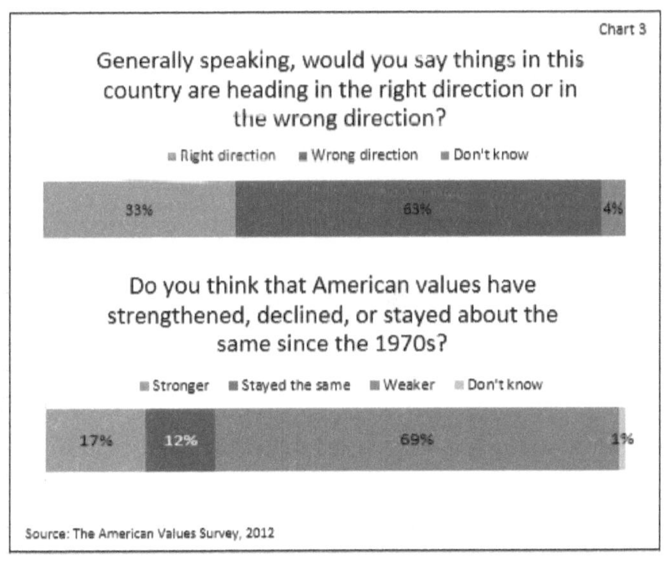

and accepted norms play a role in the moral fabric of today's society, for the purposes of this paper the focus will remain on the most relevant and significant social issues that affect the topic at hand.

Deteriorating Cultural Values and Societal Norms - Bullying

Bullying has been a part of life since the beginning of time due to limited resources, competition, and social hierarchy; however, it remains a pertinent issue that is growing and evolving as cultural values change and the scope of the problem expands. America is a highly competitive culture and that is progressively reflected in the cut-throat corporate world and in the political arena. As a result of a struggling economy, the competitive nature of our society has increased over time and is also now reinforced on the 24-hour news cycle and being constantly ingrained through things like political opposition. If children learn social norms from their parents and their surroundings – and social norms predict behavior, then it is only natural that children absorb the message of "dog eat dog" and behave accordingly. Overtime society has shifted in what it values and this reverberates in our youth. According to USA Today, the trend is more of an emphasis on extrinsic values such as money, fame, and image - and less emphasis on intrinsic values such as self-acceptance, group affiliation, and community (Healy, 2012). Now that materialistic goals are the priority, norms have shifted towards greed and there is less regard for the feelings of others.

The historical rate of bullying is difficult to define as the types and methods of bullying continue to transform. The progression of technology, often considered an advancement to human effectiveness, by default has

increased the breadth and reach of bullying victims.

Prior to cell phones and social media, bullying only

happened during face-to-face exchanges, which were

limited to the amount of free time children had during

the school day or in extracurricular activities.

Technology not only enables bullying through indirect

(non face-to-face) contact, it often facilitates anonymity

and allows bullying to occur 24-hours a day, often on

public platforms.

Regardless of the method employed, the effects of

bullying have been extensively researched and there is

great cause for concern in the short- and long-term. As

Mario Piacentini, a policy analyst at the OECD, stated,

"Bullying is very strongly related to psychological

distress and it's not just one point in time – it lasts for

life" (OECD, 2017). The OECD defines bullying as a systemic abuse of power – including physical, verbal, and relational (social exclusion). Bullying, whether as bullies, victims, or bully-victims (those who bully and who are also bullied), is associated with poor outcomes. Involvement in bullying leads to worse psychosocial adjustment, greater health problems, and poorer emotional and social adjustment (Vanderbilt & Augustyn, 2010). Long-term consequences of being bullied as a child include psychosis, depression, anxiety, poor self-esteem, and abusive relationships. The bully-victim is at the highest risk for poor outcomes with higher rates of depression, anxiety, and antisocial personality disorders, loneliness, alcohol use, poorer peer relationships, and weapon carrying (they often see justification in bringing a weapon to school). (Vanderbilt & Augustyn, 2010).

Bullying affects anywhere from 9% to 54% of youth depending on the year of the study and the cultural contexts considered when defining bullying within each study (Vanderbilt & Augustyn, 2010). The 2015 PISA study found that around 4% of students (or about one per class) reported being hit or pushed at least a few times per month. On average, 11% of students reported that they are frequently (at least a few times per month) made fun of; 7% reported that they are frequently left out of things; and 8% reported that they are frequently the object of rumors in school - possibly associated with the rise of cyberbullying (OECD, 2017) (Chart 4). Nearly 43% of kids have been bullied online;

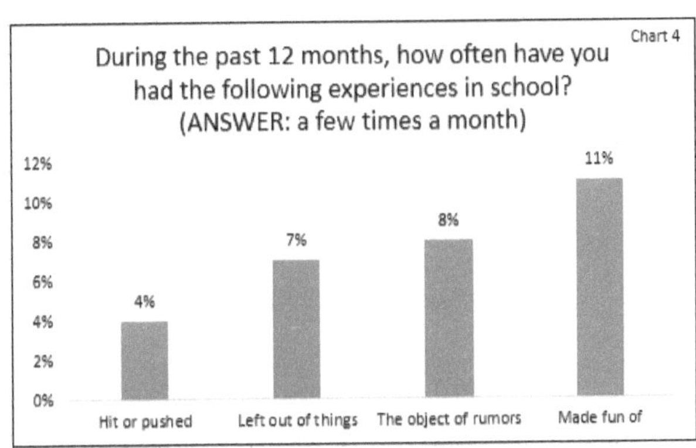

and 1 in 4 say that it has happened more than once (Moessner, 2007). More than a quarter of frequently bullied students reported relatively low satisfaction with life, compared to 10% of students who said they were not frequently bullied (OECD, 2017).

Deteriorating Cultural Values and Societal Norms - Family Life/Child Rearing

Another cultural shift that affects the development, and thus the well-being, of children is the amount of family time and positive interactions with supportive adults. Due, in part, to changes in traditional family structures, today's American families likely feature two full-time

working parents, who, when are not working, are often

preoccupied with household chores, bills, and other

responsibilities. In fact, according to the Center for

American Progress, nearly two-thirds of American

moms these days (64.4%) are breadwinners; a vast leap

from 1970, when roughly a quarter could claim that title

(Paquette, 2016). Parents often feel guilty for not

spending enough quality time with their children;

surveys show that at least half of working mothers and

fathers say they are stressed out about work-life balance

and how much time they spend with their families

(Stillman, 2017; Campbell, 2015).

As a result of feeling inattentive, parents

overcompensate by trying to shield their children from

adverse situations (Peter, 2013). Efforts to protect

children actually insulate them from healthy risk-taking behavior and it has a negative effect. Kids need to fall a few times to learn it is normal. Although parents want their children to be happy (Lyubomirsky, 2009), well-meaning adults have been shown to unknowingly limit children's access to the full range of experiences and emotions needed to build and sustain happiness, well-being, and resilience (Brussoni, Olsen, Pike, & Sleet, 2012; Cohn, Fredrickson, Brown, Mikels, & Conway, 2009; Fattore, Mason, & Watson, 2007; Fredrickson & Branigan, 2005; Ungar, 2009). If parents remove these learning opportunities from children's lives, they remove the need for children to navigate hardships and solve problems on their own and it will likely result in high arrogance and low self-esteem in our growing youth (Caprino, 2014). The book "Trophy Kids" by Ron Alsop discusses how many young people have been rewarded

for minimal accomplishments (such as mere

participation) in competitive sports, and have unrealistic

expectations of working life (Alsop, 2008). When

unmerited praise is given and/or when poor behavior is

disregarded, children eventually learn to cheat,

exaggerate, and lie to avoid difficult reality because they

have not been conditioned to effectively cope with

emotionally conflicting situations. As a natural reaction,

people tend to externalize when they encounter

problems. Without accountability, kids blame others for

their actions, refuse to follow rules they find unfair, and

find ways to justify their behavior. When there is a

missing link between choice and consequence, children

fail to cognitively assume responsibility, resulting in a

false sense of victimization. There is an imaginary line

between victimization and accountability and it is very thin (Connors, Smith, & Hickman, 2004).

Coping/Resiliency

Learning to cope with manageable threats is critical for the development of resilience. Only 37% of Americans think that children are emotionally healthy and able to cope well in adverse situations (American Humane Association, 2015). Resilience is the human ability to adapt in the face of tragedy, trauma, adversity, hardship, and ongoing significant life stressors (Newman, 2005). Some children develop resilience while others do not. The interaction between biology and environment builds a child's ability to cope with adversity and overcome threats to healthy development. According to the Center on the Developing Child at Harvard University, the single most common factor for children who develop resilience is at least one stable and committed relationship with a supportive parent, caregiver, or other adult ("Resilience," n.d.). Research indicates that condition may not be a simple one to meet. Only 39% of adults agree or strongly agree that children in America have more than one adult who is unconditionally crazy about them and positively involved in their lives (American Humane Association, 2015). In addition to the trials precipitated by the dual-parent working family, other contemporary family structure types and situations also hinder the probability that children have the support they need to develop resilience. For example, about one in four (or 24% of) fathers of children 17 or younger are living apart from at least one of their children (Livingston, 2018) and an estimated 2.7 million (or 1 in 28) have a parent in jail or prison (The Pew Charitable

Trusts, 2010). Of the parents who do live with their

children, they report spending an average of only 38.5

minutes per week in meaningful conversations with them

(Schulz, 2013).

Deteriorating Cultural Values and Societal Norms -

Media Use

Media use is a cultural value change that amplifies the

shift away from family (intrinsic) values and towards

material (extrinsic) values. The term "media" is used to

collectively describe the means of mass communication

through technological devices (i.e. television, cell

phones, iPads, social media). The progression of media

in adolescents' lives today is an example of how

technology is expediting consumption. For example, in

2011, 36% of teens had a smartphone and by 2014, 79%

of teens had a smartphone ("Facts and TV Statistics,"

n.d.). In spite of the vast range of media devices available, television continues to be a media source regularly used by Americans. 50% of adults polled in 2017 reported they often get their news on television (Bialik & Matsa, 2017). Similar television viewing habits can been seen in adolescents. An international survey found that 93% of students who attend school and live in areas with electricity have regular access to television and watch television at least 50% more than they do other out of school activities (including doing homework, being with friends, and reading) (von Feilitzen, 1998). Adolescents are also playing more video games now than ever. 97% of teens (ages 12-17) play computer, web, portable, or console games; and 50% played games "yesterday" (Lenhart et al., 2008). Children in the 1980s averaged 4 hours of video gaming per week (Gentile & Anderson, 2003), whereas today's

generation averages 13 hours per week, with boys 8 to

18 averaging 19 hours per week (Martin & Oppenheim,

2007). The use of social media is also growing,

especially as a news source for Americans overs 50

years old. The 2017 study found that two-thirds of

Americans (67%) get at least some news on social media

and more than half (55%) of Americans ages 50 and over

reported getting news on social media sites, a 10-

percentage point jump over the previous year (Bialik &

Matsa, 2017). According to the Pew Research Center,

the percentage of American adults using social media

increased from 7% to 65% between 2005 and 2015.

Among young adults (ages 18-29), the increase was even

more substantial – nine in 10 (90%) reported using social

media in 2015, compared to 12% in 2005 (Perrin, 2015)

(Chart 5). When all types of media sources are

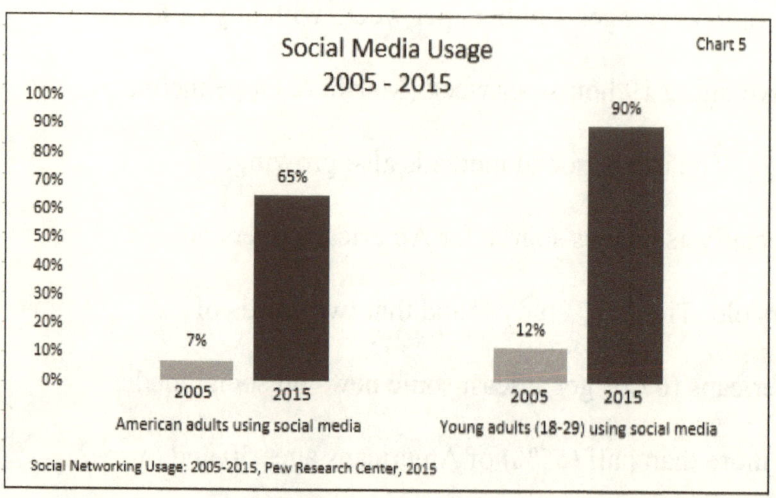

combined, studies show that tweens (8-12 years old) and

teens (13-18 years old) spend anywhere from eight to 11

hours using media per day (Wallace, 2015; Strasburger

& Hogan, 2013; Kaiser Family Foundation, 2010).

Despite America's high reliance on media use and the

number of hours that adolescents are permitted to spend

using media per day, adults are apprehensive about the

influences that the exposure may have on youth. They

report being "very concerned" or "extremely concerned"

about the absence of good adult supervision (86%), the

absence of positive attention by adults (83%), about

bullying (73%), cyberbullying (67%), social isolation

(64%), violent video games (50%), violent TV (50%),

and violent movies (49%) (American Humane

Association, 2015). One study revealed that heavy

television use is related to a more negative overall

appraisal of the quality of one's life (Morgan, 1984).

More specifically, children watching high levels of

television are less likely to experience feelings of

contentment, to participate in after-school activities, to

engage actively in other intellectually stimulating

activities, to have mostly "A" or "B" grades, and to do

well on math achievement tests (Kaiser Family

Foundation, 2010). More than half of parents (58%) say

that they worry about the influence of social media on

their child's physical and mental health (APA, 2017).

Research suggests that these concerns may be valid. In

the 2017 Stress in America Survey, 36% of Millennials

said that "social media has helped me find my identity,"

63% said "I feel like I'm attached to my phone or

tablet," 45% agreed that "even when my family is

together, I feel disconnected from them," and 38%

reported that "technology is a source of conflict in my

home." (See Chart 6 to see how Millennials compared to

other generations).

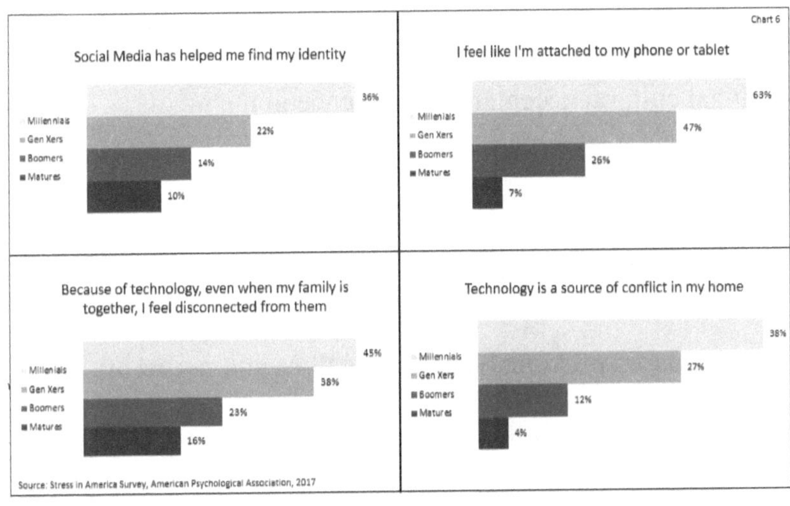

Nearly one-fifth of Americans (18%) identify the use of

technology as a very or somewhat significant source of

stress (APA, 2017). Another study found that Facebook

use predicts declines in the two components of

subjective well-being: how people feel moment to

moment and how satisfied they are with their lives

(Kross et al., 2013). The high volume use of media is

indicative of a cultural shift away from intrinsic values

and towards extrinsic values; however, an even more critical cultural acceptance is violence in the media.

Deteriorating Cultural Values and Societal Norms - Violence in the Media

As discussed previously, cultural values and norms are responsible for shaping individual behavior, including the use of violence. Media plays a major role in the development of cultural orientations, world views, and beliefs (von Feilitzen, 1998) and considering what is known about social-cognitive learning theories, violence in the media is arguably the most distressing of the accepted societal norms. There is 85 years of research on the effects of media violence on youth and although numerous governmental and nongovernmental health science organization reports all show harmful effects of media violence exposure (e.g. Payne Fund Studies, 1933;

U.S. Surgeon General's Scientific Advisory Committee, 1972; National Institute of Mental Health, 1982; Huston et al, 1992; ; Eron, Gentry, & Schlegel, 1994; Anderson et al., 2003), many people remain either unaware of, or unconvinced by, the findings. The most recent complete meta-analysis of media violence effects was conducted by Anderson and Bushman (2002). The study found that despite the research design utilized (laboratory experiments, field experiments, cross-sectional correlational studies, and longitudinal studies), the same basic effect resulted and one clear conclusion drawn: violent media exposure increases the likelihood of aggressive behavior.

Social-Cognitive Learning Models and Media

Violence

In psychology, aggression is a well-defined scientific

concept. Human aggression researchers define

aggression as a) a behavior that is intended to harm

another individual, b) the behavior is expected by the

perpetrator to have some chance of actually harming that

individual, and c) the perpetrator believes that the target

individual is motivated to avoid the harm (e.g., Anderson

& Bushman, 2002; Baron & Richardson, 1994;

Berkowitz, 1993; Geen, 2001). Violence typically is

defined by behavioral scientists as physical aggression

that is so severe that the target is likely to suffer serious

physical injury. Media violence refers to media

depictions of aggressive and violent behavior directed at

characters in the media story. Those characters can be

human or nonhuman, cartoonish or visually realistic.

Social tolerance of violent behavior is learned in

childhood, through the use of corporal punishment

(Lansford & Dodge, 2008) or witnessing violence in the

family (Abrahams & Jewkes, 2005; Brookmeyer,

Henrich, & Schwab-Stone, 2005), in the media (Johnson,

Cohen, Smailes, Kasen, & Brook, 2002) or in other

social settings. Children begin imitating and learning

from others at a very young age. As seen in Bandura's

studies, children readily imitate aggressive behaviors

they see others perform, either live or from televised

images. Children are more likely to imitate a behavior

that is followed by a reward than a behavior that is

followed by a punishment; however, aggression that was

unpunished was copied as much as aggression that was

rewarded (Bandura, 1965; Bandura, Ross, & Ross,

1963). The discovery of the mirror neuron system provides a specific physiological system for such imitative learning (e.g., Rizzolatti & Craighero, 2004). Observing and imitating other people's behavior is one of the most important sources involved in the development of a young child's motor and social skills. Children observe social interactions and their consequences from numerous sources: parents, peers, older siblings, and even fictional characters portrayed in the media. With time, children learn how to behave in certain situations and develop a set of rules for behaviors in specific events (*see discussion on Cultural Values and Norms, above*).

The General Aggression model accounts for a wide variety of effects seen in the media violence literature including both short-term and long-term effects on aggressive thoughts, feelings, and behaviors; on

emotional desensitization to violence and subsequent
declines in prosocial behavior; and on changes in the
social environment that occur as the developing child
becomes more habitually aggressive. The General
Aggression Model, as well as social learning theories,
predict that seeing what happens after an aggressive
media act can change the effect on the viewer of such
exposure. An aggressive act followed by a lack of
consequences, or even a reward, is more likely to
enhance future aggression than an aggressive act
followed by a punishment (Gentile et al., 2007). Keep
these findings in mind in the following sections.

Statistics on Media Violence

The National Television Violence Study (NTVS)
observed 23 American broadcast and cable channels over
a 20-week period (NTVS; Wilson et al., 1997, 1998).

Overall, 61% of all television programming contained some violence (while only 4% had an anti-violence theme). This percentage of violent programming increased to 81% for prime time and for Saturday morning time slots. In fact, children's programs on Saturday mornings are the most violent genre with violent acts occurring an average of 20 times in a one hour period (Brown & Hamilton-Giachritsis, 2005). Research has shown that children's cartoons have the highest frequency of television violence (Howitt & Cumberbatch, 1975; NTVS, 1997) and cartoon violence can have the same types of effects as more realistic or graphic violence (Anderson et al., 2007; Carnagey & Anderson, 2004; Liss, Reinhardt, and Fredriksen, 1983; Silvern & Williamson, 1987.). The average American child is estimated to have seen 8,000 simulated murders and over 200,000 acts of violence on TV alone by the time he or she is graduated from high school (Huston et al., 1992).

The NTVS survey found that violence in realistic settings was shown in 55% of programs, but only 16% showed long-term negative consequences and in 45% of programs, the offender went unpunished, which teaches that violence is an effective means of resolving conflict. Of further concern was that in 71% of scenes, there was no criticism of or remorse for the violence and 42% of the violence was associated with humor. Lethal violence was shown in 54% of programs, which was committed by attractive people in 39% of cases (NTVS, 1997, 1998). In American "reality-based" police shows, 87% of the criminal suspects are associated with violent crimes; however, in actuality, only 13% of crimes are violent (Oliver, 1994). By exaggerating the frequency and intensity of violence, television normalizes a distorted and misrepresented culture of violence in its viewers.

Study Results

In the first international survey conducted on children and media violence, answers to a standardized set of 60 questions inquiring upon media behavior, habits, preferences, and social environments, showed a fascination with aggressive media heroes, especially among boys. Arnold Schwarzenegger's 'Terminator' is a global icon, known by 88% of the children surveyed, be they from India, Brazil, or Japan (von Feilitzen, 1998). The study also found a remarkable number of children (44%) report a strong overlap in what they perceive as reality and what they see on the screen. Perceived realism of television violence is a predictor of later

aggression (Huesmann, Moise-Titus, Podolski, & Eron,

2003). Many children are surrounded by an environment

where "real" and media experiences both support the

view that violence is natural (von Feilitzen, 1998).

Biological or genetic factors can also increase one's

vulnerability to stress (Gershoff, Aber, & Raver, 2003).

These are significant findings, as research on vulnerable

groups has shown that some children and adolescents are

more susceptible to media influence than others based on

their cognitive appraisal and physical and social

environments (Browne & Pennell, 2000; Dorr &

Kovanic, 1981; Hopf, 2001; von Feilitzen, 1998). These

findings imply that children who view violence in the

media as an appropriate means of conflict resolution and

also observe violence as a way to solve problems in their

social environments (e.g. between their parents), are at an exponentially higher risk of displaying aggressive behavior. Cultural acceptance of violence, either as a normal method of resolving conflict or as a usual part of rearing a child, is a risk factor for all types of interpersonal violence (World Health Organization, 2002). As a result of their study, UNESCO formulated the 'compass theory,' which posits that depending on a child's already existing experiences, values, and the cultural environment, media content offers an orientation, a frame of reference which determines the direction of one's own behavior (von Feilitzen, 1998).

There is consistent evidence that violent imagery in television, film, video, and computer games has substantial short-term effects on arousal, thoughts, and emotions – increasing the likelihood of aggressive or fearful behavior in younger children (Brown &

Hamilton-Giachritsis, 2005) and also long-term effects

that are predictive of aggressive and antisocial behavior

in adulthood, even when controlling for socioeconomic

status, intelligence quotient, and various parenting

factors (Johnson et al., 2002; Huesmann et al., 2003).

Most studies show that the relationship between media

violence and real violence is interactive and cyclical;

meaning the media contributes to an aggressive culture,

and people who are already aggressive use the media as

further confirmation of their beliefs and attitudes, which

are then reinforced through media content. For example

in the UNESCO study, close to one third of the group

living in high-aggression environments thought that most

people in the world are evil, a perception reinforced by

media content (von Feilitzen, 1998). This group of

people witnessed violence in their social environments

and in the media, an everyday cycle that fortifies

opinions and beliefs and ultimately establishes a frame

of reference of the world and the people within it. This

world concept informs decisions and predicts actions

based on norms, or observed and learned methods of

acceptable behavior.

Violent Video Games

The impact of media violence can generally be explained

by the fact that aggressive behavior is more

systematically rewarded than more diplomatic ways of

coping with adversity. It is often presented as gratuitous,

thrilling, and is interpreted as a good problem-solver in a

variety of situations (von Feilitzen, 1998). The most

obvious example of how violence is construed as

rewarding is in video games, where players get points,

advance to higher levels, and win advanced weapons and faster cars in congruence with the level of violence portrayed. Armed with virtual weapons, children spend hours in exceptionally life-like situations using violence to combat perceived threats. While many of these games are intended to represent a fantasy world, game makers strive to replicate real-life settings to keep their competitive edge in the entertainment industry, adding detail to the weapons and the carnage they reap, creating more realistic experiences and blurring the line between fantasy and reality (Wiseman, 2006; Gentile et al., 2007). Seven out of 10 children (aged 8 to 17) report playing M-rated ("Mature") video games, which include the most graphic violence (Walsh et al., 2005). Video games may warrant special concern because their effects may be bigger than other forms of media violence due to

identification with the aggressor (playing the part),
active participation (much more active than the violent
TV viewer), rehearsal of entire aggression sequence,
violence directly rewarded, repetition increases learning
(Gentile et al., 2007). Violent video games provide a
forum for learning and practicing aggressive solutions to
conflict situations. The effect of violent video games
appears to be cognitive in nature. In the short term,
playing a violent video game appears to affect
aggression by priming aggressive thoughts. Longer-term
effects are likely to be longer lasting, as well, as the
player learns and practices new aggression-related
scripts that become more and more accessible for use
when real-life conflict situations arise (Anderson & Dill,
2000).

Chapter 5: Wrapping It Up

The observational and cognitive learning theory research reveals that children learn how to behave in situations through their observation of family members, peers, and the media. Similarly, cultural values and norms are learned and reinforced throughout life by parents, teachers, mentors, peers, and others in the community. The research shows that children are more likely to imitate a behavior that is followed by a reward than a behavior that is followed by a punishment; however aggression that is unpunished is copied as much as aggression that is rewarded (Bandura, 1965; Bandura et al., 1963). Those findings are alarming, considering the high volume of media our youth are consuming. The high levels of violent media is of further concern especially due to the fact that TV violence rarely shows negative consequences and often rewards violent behavior, especially in video games. It is reasonable to argue that, even if violent media does not influence the majority of people, a small group may be particularly vulnerable to negative effects incidental to the number of other risk factors present. For example, shifts in other cultural norms such as bullying and family life also contribute to mitigating factors associated with violent behavior, such as high levels of stress and other mental disorders (depression, anxiety, antisocial personality disorder), the quality of the social environment, and coping abilities. The probability of violent behavior increases proportionately with the number of risk factors present (Saner & Ellickson, 1996). Table 1 provides a summary.

Table 1				
Theories:	Research states:	Facts from research:	Mitigating risk factors:	Behavioral output:
Observational and Cognitive Learning Theories show that children learn how to behave in situations through observation (via family, peers, media)	Children are more likely to imitate a behavior that is followed by a reward than a behavior followed by a punishment. Aggression that is unpunished is copied as much as aggression that is rewarded.	Only 16% of TV violence shows negative consequences; in 45% of programs, violence went unpunished; in 71% of scenes, there was no criticism of violence or remorse shown.	High levels of exposure to media, especially violent media	Based on culturally reinforced norms
			Low levels of quality family time	
			Violence witnessed in social environment as an effective way to resolve conflict	
			Bullying	
Cultural values and norms are learned and reinforced throughout life by parents, teachers, mentors, peers, and others in the community		In video games, violence is systematically rewarded and repetition increases learning.	No coping skills/resiliency	
			High levels of stress	
			Other mental disorders (depression, anxiety, antisocial personality disorder, etc.)	

Suggestions for future research

Media violence research is unevenly distributed in the world (von Feilitzen, 1998) with the vast majority of such research being conducted in North America, some conducted in Western Europe, Japan, and Australia, but little elsewhere (Gentile et al., 2007). Future research would benefit by expanding to include other regions of the world and to include an analysis in comparison with cultural values of each studied region. Additional research into mass shooting incidents should also examine other disciplines and theories to explain possible associations that result in violent behavior. The convergence of findings across several fields and studies solidifies conclusions and leads to more compelling arguments and solutions.

Recommendations for Solutions to Future Mass Shooting Incidents

It is difficult to consider that socially accepted cultural norms may play a pivotal role in mass school shootings; however, the theoretical framework provided in this study suggests just that. The good news is that society can gain back its power and effect change, without relying on political leaders, and work towards solutions. With the information gleaned from this study, every single person has the ability to help reduce or even eliminate at least one of the mitigating risk factors associated with negative behavioral outcomes.

Communities and societies can use these findings to provide education to families and work together to promote better standards and relationships. Schools and other social institutions can take the results of this study and attend to the fundamental psychological and social needs of children to help them establish a sense of control over their lives and develop resilience in unfavorable situations. Parents, schools, and even adolescents themselves can address bullying and resolve to stop it. Parents can consciously become more supportive and actively involved in their children's lives, they can be more cognizant of the amount and type of media their children are viewing and the possible effects related to viewing violent media. Schools can also use the information provided in this framework to conduct

threat assessments on high-risk students in order to

provide them with available resources.

Understanding the role of media in young people's lives

is essential for those concerned about promoting healthy

development of children and adolescents. And there are

numerous groups involved in children's exposure to

media violence that could make positive changes –

including children themselves, parents, media industries,

distribution networks (including broadcast, cable,

theaters, rental, and retail), and government agencies.

Policies can be designed at each of these levels to limit

media violence exposure.

Society has the ability to reconstruct cultural values and

redefine what is socially accepted. The theoretical

framework explained in this study provides all the

motivation needed to commit to transformation. Once

cultural values shift back to an intrinsic focus, behavioral

patterns can be expected to reflect that change. And the

change will echo throughout all social issues.

References

Abrahams, N., & Jewkes, R. (2005). Effects of South African men's having witnessed abuse of their mothers during childhood on their levels of violence in adulthood. *American Journal of Public Health*, 95: 1811-1816.

Alsop, R. (2008). The trophy kids grow up: How the millennial generation is shaking up the workplace. San Francisco: Jossey-Bass.

American Firearms Institute (n.d.). Important Dates in Gun History. Retrieved on March 27, 2018 from http://www.americanfirearms.org/gun-history/

American Humane Association (2015). The State of America's Children: 2015 Research Study. A Report to Congress and the Nation.

https://www.americanhumane.org/publication/the

-state-of-americas-children-2015-research-study/

(Accessed February 17, 2018).

American Psychological Association (APA) (2014).

Stress in America: The State of Our Nation.

Stress in America Survey

American Psychological Association (APA) (2017).

Stress in America: Coping with Change. Stress in

America Survey

Anderson, C.A., & Bushman, B.J. (2002). Human

aggression. *Annual Review of Psychology*, 53,

27-51.

Anderson, C.A., & Dill, K.E. (2000). Video games and

aggressive thoughts, feelings, and behavior in the

laboratory and in life. *Journal of Personality and Social Psychology, 78*, 772-790.

Anderson, C. A., Gentile, D. A., & Buckley, K. E. (2007). *Violent Video game effects on children and adolescents: Theory, research, and public policy.* New York : Oxford University Press.

Bandura, A. (1965). Influence of models' reinforcement contingencies on the acquisition of imitative responses. *Journal of Personality and Social Psychology, 1*, pp. 589-595.

Bandura, A., Ross, D., & Ross, S.A. (1963). A comparative test of the status envy, social power, and secondary reinforcement theories of identificatory learning. *Journal of Abnormal and Social Psychology, 66*, 3-11.

Baron, R.A., & Richardson, D.R. (1994). *Human aggression*. (2nd ed.). New York: Plenum.

Berkowitz, L. (1989). Frustration-aggression hypothesis: Examination and reformulation.*Psychological Bulletin*, 106, 59–73.

Berkowitz, L. (1993). *Aggression: Its causes, consequences, and control*. New York : McGraw-Hill.

Bialik, K. & Matsa, K. (2017, October 4). Key trends in social and digital news media. Pew Research Center. Retrieved on March 21, 2018 from http://www.pewresearch.org/fact-tank/2017/10/04/key-trends-in-social-and-digital-news-media/

Bornstein, R. (2006). The complex relationship between

dependency and domestic violence: Converging

psychological factors and social forces. *American

Psychologist*, 61(6), 595-606.

Brookmeyer, K.A., Henrich, C.C., & Schwab-Stone, M.

(2005). Adolescents who witness community

violence: can parent support and prosocial

cognitions protect them from committing

violence? *Child Development*, 76: 917-929.

Brown, K., & Hamilton-Giachritsis, C. (2005). The

influence of violent media on children and

adolescents: A public health approach. The

Lancet, 365(9460), 702-710.

http://dx.doi.org/10.1016/S0140-6736(05)17952-

5

Browne, K.D., & Pennell, A.E. (2000). The influence of

film and video on young people and violence. In:

Boswell G, ed. Violent children and adolescents:

asking the question why. London and

Philadelphia: Whurr, 2000: 151–68.

Brussoni, M., Olsen, L. L., Pike, I., & Sleet, D. A.

(2012). Risky play and children's safety:

Balancing priorities for optimal child

development. International Journal of

Environmental Research and Public Health, 9(9),

3134–3148. doi:10.3390/ijerph9093134

Campbell, A. (2015, November 4). How Working Moms

Are Changing American Households. The

Atlantic. Retrieved on March 19, 2018 from

https://www.theatlantic.com/politics/archive/201

5/11/how-working-moms-are-changing-

american-households/433332/

Caprino, K. (2014, January 16). 7 Crippling Parenting

Behaviors That Keep Children From Growing

Into Leaders. Forbes.com. Retrieved February

21, 2018 from

https://www.forbes.com/sites/kathycaprino/2014/

01/16/7-crippling-parenting-behaviors-that-keep-

children-from-growing-into-

leaders/#1e4482395957

Carnagey, N. L., & Anderson, C. A. (2003). Theory in

the study of media violence: The general

aggression model. In D. A. Gentile (Ed.), *Media

violence and children: A complete guide for

parents and professionals* (pp. 87–106). Westport

, CT : Praeger.

Carnagey, N., & Anderson, C. (2004). Violent video game exposure and aggression: A literature review. *Minerva Psichiatrica*, 45, 1–18.

Carnagey, N. L., Anderson, C. A., & Bushman, B. J. (2007). The effect of video game violence on physiological desensitization to real-life violence. *Journal of Experimental Social Psychology*, **43**, 489–496.

Cohn, B. (2012, June 27). 21 Charts That Explain American Values Today. The Atlantic. Retrieved on March 20, 2018 from https://www.theatlantic.com/national/archive/2012/06/21-charts-that-explain-american-values-today/258990/

Cohn, M. A., Fredrickson, B. L., Brown, S. L., Mikels, J. A., & Conway, A. M. (2009). Happiness unpacked: Positive emotions increase life satisfaction by building resilience. Emotion, 9(3), 361–368. doi:10.1037/a0015952

Connors, R., Smith, T., & Hickman, C. R. (2004). *The Oz principle: Getting results through individual and organizational accountability*. New York, N.Y: Portfolio

Dorr, A., & Kovanic, P. (1981). Some of the people, some of the time - but which people? Televised violence and its effects. In: Palmer EL, Dorr A, eds. Children and the faces of television, teaching, violence and selling. New York: Academic Press, 1981: 183–99

Facts and TV Statistics. (n.d.). Parents Television

Council. Retrieved on March 21, 2018 from

http://w2.parentstv.org/main/Research/Facts.aspx

Farah, M., Nobel, K., & Hurt, H. (2007). The developing

adolescent brain in socioeconomic context. In D.

Romer (ED.), *Adolescent psychology and the*

developing brain: Integrating brain and

prevention science (pp. 373-387). New York,

NY: Oxford University Press.

Fattore, T., Mason, J., & Watson, E. (2007). Children's

conceptualisation(s) of their well-being. Social

Indicators Research, 80(1), 5–29.

doi:10.1007/s11205- 006-9019-9

Fredrickson, B. L., & Branigan, C. (2005). Positive

emotions broaden the scope of attention and

thought-action repertoires. Cognition and Emotion, 19(3), 313–332. doi:10.1080/02699930441000238

Geen, R.G. (2001). Human aggression (2nd ed.). Philadelphia: Open University Press.

Gentile, D.A., & Anderson, C.A. (2003). Violent video games: The Newest Media Violence Hazard. Chapter in D.A. Gentile (Ed.). *Media violence and children*. Westport, CT: Praeger.

Gentile, D., Saleem, M., & Anderson, C. (2007). Public Policy and the Effects of Media Violence on Children. *Social Issues and Policy Review, in press*. https://doi-org.ezproxy.lib.uconn.edu/10.1111/j.1751-2409.2007.00003.x

Gershoff, E.T., Aber, J.L., & Raver, D.C. (2003). Child

poverty in the U.S.: An evidence-based

conceptual framework for programs and policies.

In R.M. Lerner, F. Jacobs, & D. Wertlieb (Eds.),

Handbook of Applied Developmental Science,

Vol. 2, (pp. 81-136). Thousand Oaks, CA: Sage

Publications.

Healy, M. (2012, March 15). Millennials might not be so

special after all, study finds. USAToday.com.

Retrieved March 16, 2018 from

http://usatoday30.usatoday.com/news/health/well

ness/story/2012-03-15/Millennials-might-not-be-

so-special-after-all-study-finds/53552744/1

Hopf C. (2001). Violence, biography and the media. A

qualitative study on the biographical

reasonability of violent film actions. Zeitschrift

fur Soziologie der Erziehung und Socialization

2001; 21: 150–69

Howitt, D., & Cumberbatch, G. (1975). *Mass media

violence and society*. New York : John Wiley.

Huesmann L.R., Moise-Titus, J., Podolski, C.L., & Eron,

L.D. (2003). Longitudinal relations between

children's exposure to TV violence and their

aggressive and violent behavior in young

adulthood: 1977-1992. *Developmental

Psychology*, 39(2): 201-221.

Huston, A. C., Donnerstein, E., Fairchild, H., Feshbach,

N. D., Katz, P. A., Murray, J. P., Rubinstein, E.

A., Wilcox, B. L., & Zuckernan, D. (1992). *Big

world. small screen: The role of television in*

American Society. Lincoln : University of

Nebraska Press

Johnson, J.G., Cohen, P., Smailes, E.M., Kasen, S., &
Brook, J.S. (2002). Television viewing and
aggressive behavior during adolescence and
adulthood. *Science*, 295: 2468-2471.

Kaiser Family Foundation. (2010). Generation M2:
Media in the lives of 8-to 18-year-olds. Retrieved
on March 21, 2018 from
http://www.KFF.org/entmedia/upload/8010.pdf

Kross, E., Verduyn, P., Demiralp, E., Park, J., Lee, D.,
Lin, N., Shablack, H., Jonides, J., & Ybarra, O.
(2013). Facebook Use Predicts Declines in
Subjective Well-Being in Young Adults. PLoS

ONE 8(8): e69841.

https://doi.org/10.1371/journal.pone.0069841

Lansford, J.E., & Dodge, K.A. (2008). Cultural norms for adult corporal punishment of children and societal rates of endorsement and use of violence. *Parenting: Science and Practice*, 8: 257-270.

Lenhart, A., Kahne, J., Middaugh, E., Macgill, A., Evans, C., & Vitak, J. (2008, September 16). Teens, Video Games and Civics. Pew Research Center. Retrieved on 3/21/18 from http://www.pewinternet.org/2008/09/16/teens-video-games-and-civics/

Liss, M. B., Reinhardt, L. C., & Fredriksen, S. (1983). TV heroes: The impact of rhetoric and deeds.*Journal of Applied Developmental Psychology*, 4, 175–187.

Livingston, G. (2018). Most dads say they spend too little time with their children; about a quarter live apart from them. Pew Research Center. PewResearch.org. Accessed February 28, 2018 from http://www.pewresearch.org/fact-tank/2018/01/08/most-dads-say-they-spend-too-little-time-with-their-children-about-a-quarter-live-apart-from-them/

Lyubomirsky, S. (2009). The how of happiness: Is it possible to become lastingly happier and if so, how? Paper presented at the Happiness & Its Causes Conference, Sydney, Australia.

Martin, S. & Oppenheim, K. (2007). Video gaming:

General and pathological use. *Trends & Tudes*,

6(3), 1-7.

McLeod, S. (2014). Bobo Doll Experiment. Simply

Psychology. Retrieved on March 20, 2018 from

https://www.simplypsychology.org/bobo-

doll.html

Mental Illness. (n.d.). National Institute of Mental Health

(NIH). Retrieved on March 19, 2018 from

https://www.nimh.nih.gov/health/statistics/menta

l-illness.shtml

Moessner, C. (2007). Cyberbullying, Trends and Tudes.

NCPC.org. Accessed March 16, 2018 from

http://www.ncpc.org/resources/files/pdf/bullying/

Cyberbullying%20Trends%20-%20Tudes.pdf.

Morgan, M. (1984). Heavy Television Viewing and

Perceived Quality of Life." *Journalism

Quarterly*, 61, 499-504.

National Television Violence Study. (1997). *Technical

Report, 2*. Thousand Oaks, CA:Sage.

National Television Violence Study. (1998). *Technical

Report, 2*. Thousand Oaks, CA:Sage.

Newman, R. (2005). APA's Resilience Initiative.

Professional Psychology: Research And Practice,

36(3), 227-229. doi:10.1037/0735-7028.36.3.227

OECD (2017), *PISA 2015 Results (Volume V):

Collaborative Problem Solving*, OECD

Publishing, Paris.

http://dx.doi.org/ID.1787/9789264285521-en

Oliver, M. (1994). Portrayals of Crime, Race and

Aggression in "Reality Based" Police Shows: A

Content Analysis. *Journal of Broadcasting and*

Electronic Media, 38(2), 179-192.

Paquette, D. (2016, December 22). The days of stay-at-

home moms are 'long gone,' data show. The

Washington Post. Retrieved on March 26, 2018

from

https://www.washingtonpost.com/news/wonk/wp

/2016/12/22/the-days-of-stay-at-home-moms-are-

long-gone-data-show/?utm_term=.63ac0c7ac725

Penn, M. (2012, June 27). Americans Are Losing

Confidence in the Nation but Still Believe in

Themselves. The Atlantic. Retrieved on March

20, 2018 from

https://www.theatlantic.com/national/archive/201

2/06/americans-are-losing-confidence-in-the-

nation-but-still-believe-in-themselves/259039/

Perrin, A. (2015, October 8). Social Media Usage: 2005-

2015. Pew Research Center.

www.pewresearch.org. Retrieved on February

28, 2018 from

http://www.pewinternet.org/2015/10/08/2015/So

cial-Networking-Usage-2005-2015/

Peter, M. (2013, July 30). The over compensating parent.

Retrieved on March 27, 2018 from

http://www.parent24.com/Child_7-

12/Development/The-over-compensating-parent-

20130726

Resilience. (n.d.). Center on the Developing Child,

Harvard University. Retrieved on February 21,

2018 from

https://developingchild.harvard.edu/science/key-concepts/resilience/

Rizzolatti, G., & Craighero, L. (2004). The mirror-neuron system. *Annual Review of Neuroscience, 27*, 169-192.

Rosmond, R. (2005). Role of the pathogenesis of the metabolic syndrome. *Psychoneuroendocrinology, 30*(1), 1-10.

Saner, H. & Ellickson, P. (1996). Concurrent risk factors for adolescent violence. *Journal of Adolescent Health*, 19(2), 94-103.

Schulz, J. (2013, September 9). The value of family meal time. Michigan State University. Retrieved on March 19, 2018 from

http://msue.anr.msu.edu/news/the_value_of_fami

ly_meal_time

Silvern, S. B., & Williamson, P. A. (1987). The effects

of video game play on young children's

aggression, fantasy, and prosocial

behavior. *Journal of Applied Developmental

Psychology*, 8, 453–462.

Steinberg, L. (2005). *Adolescence* (7th ed.). New York,

NY: McGraw-Hill.

Stillman, J. (2017, November 14). Science to Guilty

Parents: Stop Stressing Out About Spending

'Quality Time' With Your Kids. Inc.com.

Retrieved on March 19, 2018 from

https://www.inc.com/jessica-stillman/science-to-guilty-parents-stop-stressing-out-about-spending-

quality-time-with-your-kids.html

Strasburger, V. C. & Hogan, M. J. (2013). Children,

Adolescents, and the Media. *Journal of*

Pediatrics, 132(5), 958-961.

doi:10.1542/peds.2013-2656

The Pew Charitable Trusts: Pew Center on the States.

Collateral Costs: Incarceration's Effect on

Economic Mobility. Washington, DC. 2010

Ungar, M. (2009). Overprotective parenting: Helping

parents provide children the right amount of risk

and responsibility. American Journal of Family

Therapy, 37(3), 258–271.

doi:10.1080/01926180802534724

Vanderbilt, & Augustyn. (2010). The effects of

bullying. *Paediatrics and Child Health, 20*(7),

315-320.

von Feilitzen, C. (1998). Introduction. U. Carlsson, & C.

von Feilitzen (Eds), Children and media violence

(pp. 45-54). Goteborg, Sweden: The UNESCO

International Clearinghouse Media Violence 78

on Children and Violence on the Screen.

Wallace, K. (2015, November 3). Teens spend a 'mind-

boggling' 9 hours a day using media, report says.

CNN.com. Retrieved on February 28, 2018 from

https://www.cnn.com/2015/11/03/health/teens-

tweens-media-screen-use-report/index.html

Walsh, D., Gentile, D., Walsh, E., Bennett, N.,

Robideau, B., Walsh, M., Strikland, S., &

McFadden, D. (2005). *Tenth annual MediaWise video game report card*. Minneapolis, MN: National Institute on Media and the Family. http://www.mediafamily.org/research/report_vgr c_2005.shtml

Wilson, B. J., Kunkel, D., Linz, D., Potter, J., Donnerstein, E., Smith, S. L., Blumenthal, E., & Gray, T. (1997). Violence in television programming overall: University of California, Santa Barbara study. In M. Seawall. (Ed.), *National television violence study* (Vol. 1, pp. 3–184). Thousand Oaks , CA : Sage Publications.

Wilson, B. J., Kunkel, D., Linz, D., Potter, J., Donnerstein, E., Smith, S. L., Blumenthal, E., & Berry, M. (1998). Violence in television programming overall: University of California,

Santa Barbara study. In M. Seawall

(Ed.), *National television violence study* (Vol. 2,

pp. 3–204). Thousand Oaks , CA : Sage

Publications.

Wiseman, M. (2006). Literature Review on Media

Violence, Children and Small Arms. SEESAC.

Retrieved on February 28, 2018 from

http://www.seesac.org/f/docs/SALW-and-

ChildrenYouth/Literature-Review-on-Media-

Violence-Children-and-Small-Arms-EN.pdf

World report on violence and health: summary. Geneva,

World Health Organization, 2002.

<u>About the Author</u>

Meagin Colson has been interested in criminal behavior since she was a young child, evidenced by the fact that Dragnet was her favorite TV show. This curiosity led her double majoring in Criminology and Psychology at Florida State University and landing a job in law enforcement soon after graduating. She worked as a homicide analyst for many years while simultaneously earning her Master's Degree in Forensic Psychology from the Chicago School of Professional Psychology. The past four years she has been doing research and strategic planning at the same law enforcement agency she started at 13 years ago. She recently completed a Master's program in Survey Research at the University of Connecticut. In her spare time, Meagin researches the human brain/mind, behavior, consciousness, physics, quantum physics, geometry, astronomy, biology, etc –

and their inter-relatedness. Meagin is married to a 20-

year law enforcement veteran, has a 14 year-old step-

daughter, and two beloved dogs.